Fossils

By Kris Hirschmann

World Discovery Science Readers™

SCHOLASTIC INC.

New York • Toronto • London • Auckland • Sydney
Mexico City • New Delhi • Hong Kong • Buenos Aires

Fossil remains of a prehistoric bat

Chapter 1

What Are Fossils?

No one is sure when life began on Earth. But plants and animals have been here for hundreds of millions of years. How do we know this? Because of **fossils**.

Fossils are the preserved remains of plants and animals. They are clues to our planet's past. Scientists study fossils because they are trying to learn about **prehistoric** times.

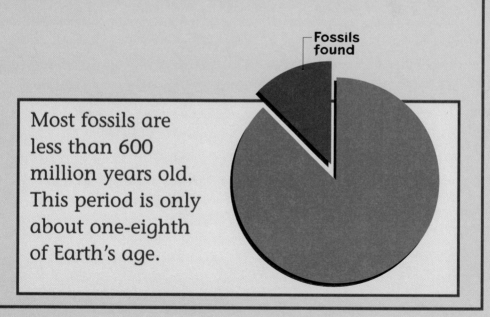

Fossils found

Most fossils are less than 600 million years old. This period is only about one-eighth of Earth's age.

Most fossils formed after animals or plants fell into a soft substance like mud or tar. **Sediment,** which is found at the bottom of the ocean, a lake, or a pond, also helped preserve fossils. The animals or plants sank into the mushy substance. Eventually their soft parts—like flesh—rotted away. But their harder parts—like bones—did not rot.

Prehistoric dolphin fossil

This fish fossil was found in Wyoming.

Over many, many years, sediments fell down onto the soft substances. These sediments built up and got very heavy. They squeezed the soft substances until they turned into rocks. The animal and plant parts were trapped inside the rocks. The remains then turned into fossils.

Earth's **crust** is made of giant moving rock plates. Sometimes parts of the plates get shoved upward, and long-buried fossils reach the surface.

Edge of plate rises

Fossils appear

Plates bump together

There are many ways to tell the age of a fossil. One good way is to check the age of the rocks around the fossil. Scientists do this by measuring the rocks' radioactivity. All rocks are **radioactive**, but they lose some of their radioactivity over time. Scientists run tests to see how much radioactivity a rock has lost. This tells them the age of the rock.

Rocks build up in layers. The top layers are the youngest, and the deep layers are the oldest.

Scientists can also look at things near the fossil. They hope to find other fossilized plants or animals that only lived on Earth for a very short time. These types of fossils are called **index fossils**. Earlier radioactivity tests have already found the age of the index fossils. Scientists assume that anything nearby is about the same age.

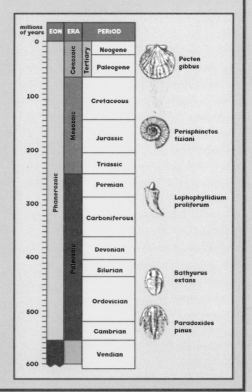

millions of years	EON	ERA	PERIOD	
0	Phanerozoic	Cenozoic	Tertiary — Neogene	Pecten gibbus
			Tertiary — Paleogene	
100		Mesozoic	Cretaceous	
200			Jurassic	Perisphinctos tiziani
			Triassic	
		Paleozoic	Permian	Lophophyllidium proliferum
300			Carboniferous	
400			Devonian	
			Silurian	Bathyurus extans
			Ordovician	
500			Cambrian	Paradoxides pinus
600			Vendian	

Fossils teach us many things about the past. One of the most important things fossils teach us is how plants and animals looked long ago. For example, the skeletons of ancient animals give us clues about the shape and size of creatures' bodies. Fossilized leaves and other plant parts let us "see" the jungles and forests that grew on Earth many millions of years ago.

Leaf fossil

Fossils also show us how Earth's surface has changed. For example, fossilized sea animals are sometimes found on dry land. This teaches us where ancient oceans were found. Sea animal remains might also be found on mountaintops. This shows us that some of Earth's tallest peaks were once underwater.

Sometimes ancient insects got stuck in tree sap. The sap hardened into **amber**. The insects' bodies were perfectly preserved inside the amber.

Ammonite fossils are ancient mollusks.

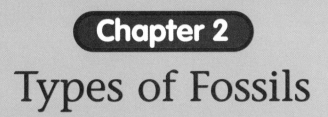

Chapter 2

Types of Fossils

All fossils start as plants or animals that get buried or make a mark on a soft substance. But once this happens, fossils form in many different ways. There are four main types of fossils. They are called **mineral fossils**, **molds**, **casts**, and **trace fossils**.

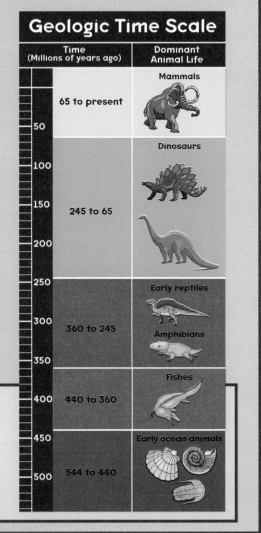

Geologic Time Scale

Time (Millions of years ago)	Dominant Animal Life
65 to present	Mammals
245 to 65	Dinosaurs
360 to 245	Early reptiles / Amphibians
440 to 360	Fishes
544 to 440	Early ocean animals

Certain types of fossils were most common during certain time periods.

Fossilized brittlestar, a marine animal

Mineral fossils are the most common type of fossil. Mineral fossils form when water touches buried bones, teeth, shells, or other hard material. The water washes away little bits of the original material. It leaves behind tiny chunks of minerals, the hard substances that make rocks. After thousands of years, all of the original material is replaced by minerals. Only a rocky fossil remains.

Hard objects that contain **pores** (tiny holes) may also become mineral fossils. Bones, shells, and sponges are some things that have pores. Water seeps into the pores and leaves minerals behind. Over time the objects turn into rocks. The rocks are the exact size and shape of the original objects.

This is a close-up picture of a sponge's pores. Minerals enter the pores and turn into rock.

Molds and casts are two other types of fossils that scientists often find. Molds are fossilized dents made by plants and animals. Molds form when an object presses into mud or another soft substance. In time, the mud hardens into rock. Then the object dissolves. The object leaves its imprint in the rock.

This fossilized tortoise is a cast found in the badlands of South Dakota. This turtle lived more than 35 million years ago.

The trilobite cast on the right has been separated from its mold on the left.

Sometimes molds fill with minerals. Over time the minerals turn into stone shapes called casts. A cast can be pulled from its mold just like an ice cube is pulled from a tray. The cast's surface shows every detail of the original object.

You can make a cast by pouring plaster of Paris into an animal track or any other dent. Remove the plaster shape after it dries.

Plaster of Paris

Animal print

Sometimes fossils form from markings or other things that animals leave behind. These fossils are called trace fossils. Footprints are one common type of trace fossil. Scientists study fossilized footprints to learn about an ancient animal's weight and size. Footprints can also tell scientists whether an animal hopped, walked, or ran.

An ancient fossilized human footprint from Nicaragua

Footprints became fossils after animals left tracks in soft substances.

This fossilized turtle dung is an example of a coprolite.

Sometimes an animal's droppings turn into fossils. Fossilized droppings are called **coprolites**. Coprolites can show us what an animal ate and where it lived.

Animal homes may even become fossils. Scientists have found fossilized termite nests in New Mexico. They have also found fossilized worm burrows in South Dakota and fossilized bee nests in Argentina. These fossils teach us about the lifestyles of animals that lived long ago.

This fossilized shrimp from Lebanon has been varnished for display purposes.

Chapter 3

Fossils on Display

Museums use fossils to teach the public about ancient times. They do this by putting the most interesting fossils on display for everyone to see.

You might see many types of fossils in a museum. But some are more common than others. The most popular fossils include dinosaur skeletons, **trilobites**, **ammonites**, and ancient plants.

Trilobites were common in prehistoric times. A group of fossilized trilobites is shown on the right.

The most complete *Tyrannosaurus rex* skeleton ever found is on display at Chicago's Field Museum. The skeleton is named Sue.

Dinosaur skeletons are the fossilized remains of some ancient reptiles and birds. The biggest dinosaurs were more than 80 feet (24.4 m) long and weighed more than 90 tons! Dinosaurs appeared on Earth about 230 million years ago. They became extinct about 65 million years ago.

Some dinosaur skeletons are made of only bone, but many are not. They may be made partly of stone, too. Minerals sometimes filled the pores in the original bony material.

The skeletons of thirty-seven different types of dinosaurs have been found in Canada's Dinosaur Provincial Park.

Dinosaur Provincial Park

Fossilized dinosaur bones have been found all over the world. One big bone site is in Montana. More than 10,000 maiasaur skeletons are buried here. Dinosaur bones have also been found in Utah as well as Canada, Tanzania, and parts of China.

Triceratops

Trilobites and ammonites are among the world's most common fossils. The remains of these animals can be found everywhere on Earth.

Trilobites lived between 570 and 245 million years ago. They are related to crabs and lobsters. There were more than 10,000 types of trilobites. Most were less than 4 inches (10 cm) long.

Tribolite fossil

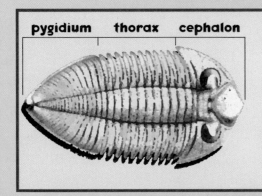

pygidium   thorax   cephalon

The word trilobite means "three parts." This diagram shows the three parts of a trilobite's body.

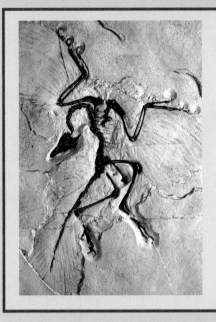

This archaeopteryx fossil was found in Germany. An archaeopteryx was a bird that lived 150 to 200 million years ago, during the Jurassic era.

But the biggest types could be 19 inches (48 cm) long. Trilobites were oval with sharply ridged backs.

Ammonites lived between 365 and 65 million years ago. These sea creatures had coiled shells that looked like a mountain goat's horns. The insides of the shells were divided into chambers. The chambers of some ammonite fossils are filled with colorful minerals.

Fossilized ammonite, showing the divided chambers within

Fossilized trees in Colorado

Some ancient plants turned into beautiful fossils. Land plants appeared about 440 million years ago. The earliest plants were no more than 1 inch (2.5 cm) tall. Within a few million years plants evolved and became much larger. Some trees that lived 350 million years ago were 100 feet (30.5 meters) tall. Their trunks were 5 feet (1.5 meters) across.

Most plant fossils are **carbon prints.** These prints were made when dead plants decayed. They left behind a dark mineral called carbon. The carbon printed perfect pictures of the dead plants onto rocks.

Fern imprints found in coal

Coal is a type of plant fossil. It is made from trees that lived millions of years ago. Today, people burn coal to create heat and energy.

Some plant fossils are so good that scientists can see every detail of the original object. This picture shows a seed that turned into charcoal during a long-ago forest fire.

Fossilized dimetrodon found in Texas

Chapter 4

Finding Fossils

Fossil hunting is exciting! Digging up a buried fossil is like finding a hidden treasure. Some people enjoy fossil hunting so much that they turn it into a career. They become fossil scientists.

Other people hunt fossils just for fun. They find small fossils and keep them in private collections. You could be one of these people!

This chart shows some of North America's best fossil-hunting sites.

Site	Place	Age
Rancho La Brea	Southern California, USA	20,000 years old
Ashfall Fossil Beds	Nebraska, USA	10 million years old
Green River Formation	Wyoming and Colorado, USA	50 million years old
Mazon Creek	Northeastern Illinois, USA	300 million years old
Burgess Shale	British Columbia, Canada	530 million years old

Paleontologist Rodolfo Coria dusts teeth on the fossil jawbone of the largest carnivorous dinosaur, *Giganotosaurus*, discovered to date, found in 1993 at El Chocon, Argentina.

People who find and study fossils for a living are called **paleontologists**. Most paleontologists **specialize** in one type of fossil. For example, some paleontologists like to look for dinosaur bones. Others collect and study trilobites or plants.

A fossil site is called a **dig**. Paleontologists remove fossils from digs with knives, small shovels, chisels, and hammers. They work slowly and carefully so they will not harm the fossils. They take pictures and draw sketches to record everything they do.

Fossils are taken to a lab after they are dug up. In the lab, scientists prepare the

fossils to be examined. They often use soft brushes to clean the fossils. Sometimes they also coat the fossils with **varnish** to protect them.

Scientists use strings to make grids over fossil digs. They work in one square at a time.

You do not have to be a scientist to collect fossils. Anyone can enjoy this fun hobby.

It is easiest to find fossils in rocky areas. Cliffs and quarries are good places to start. Areas that contain sedimentary rocks (rocks that build up in layers over time) are also good places to look. Ammonites, trilobites, and other fossils are often found in these places. Ask a parent before you visit any rocky area. They can be dangerous.

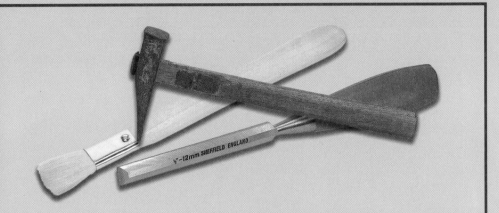

Take a small hammer, a chisel, and a brush with you to remove fossils from rocks. Always wear safety glasses when hammering. Work carefully so you don't break the fossils.

At home, use a field guide to identify the fossils you find. Then label each fossil and put it on display. Do you feel a little bit like a detective? You should. After all, you just discovered a tiny piece of Earth's history!

Display your fossils so you can enjoy them every day.

Glossary

Amber: Hardened tree sap.

Ammonites: Prehistoric sea creatures with spiral, chambered shells.

Carbon prints: Imprints left after plants decayed.

Casts: Fossils that form when minerals fill dents and harden into rocks.

Coprolites: Fossilized animal droppings.

Crust: The hard top layer of Earth.

Dig: A place where scientists are looking for fossils.

Fossils: The preserved remains of plants and animals.

Index fossils: Fossils of plants or animals that lived on Earth for a very short time.

Mineral fossils: Fossils created after the original object is replaced over time by minerals.

Molds: Fossilized dents made by plants and animals.

Paleontologist: A scientist who studies fossils.

Pores: Tiny holes.

Prehistoric: Before recorded history.

Radioactive: Giving off energy particles.

Sediment: Fine matter like dirt or silt.

Specialize: To focus on one narrow topic or field.

Trace fossils: Fossils made from markings or other things that animals leave behind.

Trilobites: Prehistoric relatives of crabs and lobsters.

Varnish: A clear liquid that dries into a hard coating.